A first guide to
INSECTS

SIMON PERRY

Illustrated by
Cecilia Fitzsimons

HODDER AND STOUGHTON
LONDON SYDNEY AUCKLAND TORONTO

For Rachel

British Library Cataloguing in Publication Data
Perry, Simon
  A first guide to insects.
  1. Insects
  I. Title   II. Fitzsimons, Cecilia
  595.7

  ISBN 0-340-53106-1

Text copyright © Simon Perry 1991
Artwork copyright © Cecilia Fitzsimons 1991

First published 1991

The author's and publishers' thanks are due to
the following for permission to reproduce photographs:
(l) = left
(r) = right
Heather Angel cover, 10, 12, 14, 15, 18(r), 25(l);
Aquila Photographics Ltd/Abraham Cardwell 20 (r),
/Tom Leach 11,/Duncan I McEwan 8, 23,
/Robert Maier 18(l), 20(l), 27,/C.S. Milkins 13,
/R.T. Mills title page, 16,/R. Siegel 25(r); Ardea/John Mason 22,
/P. Morris 26; Ron & Christine Foord 17, 24.

All rights reserved. No part of this publication may be reproduced or transmitted in any form or by any means, electronically or mechanically, including photocopying, recording, or any information storage and retrieval system, without either prior permission in writing from the publisher or a licence permitting restricted copying. In the United Kingdom such licences are issued by the Copyright Licensing Agency, 33-34 Alfred Place, London WC1E 7DP.

The rights of Simon Perry to be identified as author of the text of this work and of Cecilia Fitzsimons to be identified as the illustrator of this work have been asserted by them in accordance with the Copyright, Designs and Patents Act 1988.

Published by Hodder and Stoughton Children's Books, a division of Hodder and Stoughton Ltd, Mill Road, Dunton Green, Sevenoaks, Kent TN13 2YA

Design by Katrina ffiske

Printed in Belgium by Proost International Book Production

Contents

Note to Parents and Teachers	*4*
Introduction	*5*
Grasshoppers and friends	8
Dragonflies and Mayflies	10
Land Bugs	12
Water Bugs	14
Butterflies	16
Moths	18
Flies	20
Bees, Wasps and Ants	22
Larger Beetles	24
Smaller Beetles	26
Activities	*28*
Index	*32*

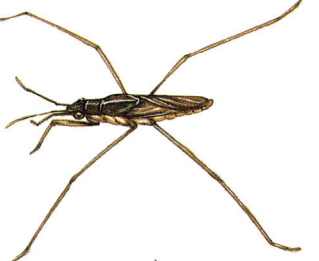

Note to Parents and Teachers

Throughout the world, there are more species of insect than of all other animal species put together. In the British Isles alone, scientists have identified more than 20,000 different insect types. Identification is helped by the fact that insects are grouped according to features they have in common. There are over thirty such groups, and some group names – for example, butterfly, beetle and wasp – are familiar to most children.

The insects in this book have been selected from the eleven groups of insects children are most likely to come across. These are: bristletails; springtails; mayflies; dragonflies; crickets and grasshoppers; earwigs; true bugs; butterflies and moths; bees, wasps and their allies; true flies; and beetles. The insects are not only among the most common, but also the most representative of their groups. This means that if a child spots a common butterfly, such as the large white (which is not illustrated), the section on butterflies should enable him or her to see that it is closely related to the small white (which is illustrated).

To help children find the insects included in this book, each group of insects has been given symbols which describe the insects' normal habitats. These are –

 woodland: *small woods or large forests*

 grassland – including over-grown areas in towns

 hedgerows

 crop fields

 town parks

 inside buildings

 gardens

 beside water: *ponds, streams and rivers*

Many young children are fascinated by mini-beasts and learn most about them through their own discoveries. This book is not a substitute for exploration, but a starting point. Encourage children to try the activities on pages 28 to 31, and to use the book as a guide to field identification.

The majority of insects are not pests. In fact, many are helpful or at least, harmless. Yet, the use of pesticides and the disappearance of many wildlife habitats means that many insects are threatened with extinction. With this book, encourage children better to understand and perhaps marvel at the wonderful world of insects, and so help them to develop a concern for their care and conservation.

Introduction

Insect or mini-beast?

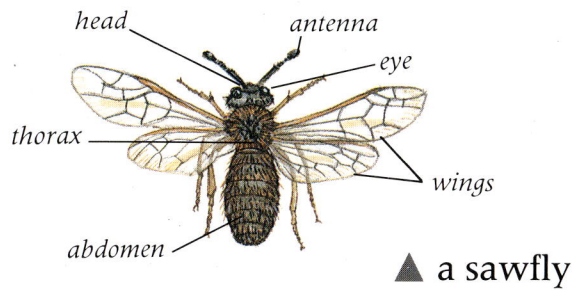

▲ a sawfly

This is a typical insect. It has a body with three sections, six legs, and two pairs of wings. The legs and wings are connected to the middle part of the body, called the thorax. At the front is the head, with two feelers called antennae. At the back is the abdomen. On some insects it is difficult to see all three parts. Some young insects, called larvae, may have more or fewer than six legs. They have no wings; only adult insects have wings. Even then, true flies have only one pair, and some insects have none.

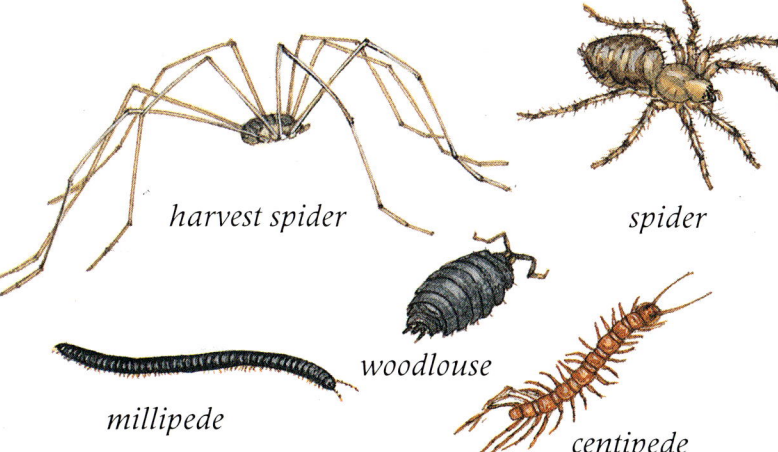

No other mini-beast can fly. Centipedes and millipedes have many more legs. Woodlice have seven pairs of legs, while anything with four pairs of legs belongs to the spider family.

Insect parts

Although all insects have the same basic parts, the parts are not exactly the same in every insect. This is because insects live in different places and feed on different things. Can you discover who owns these wings and legs? Look through the book to find out.

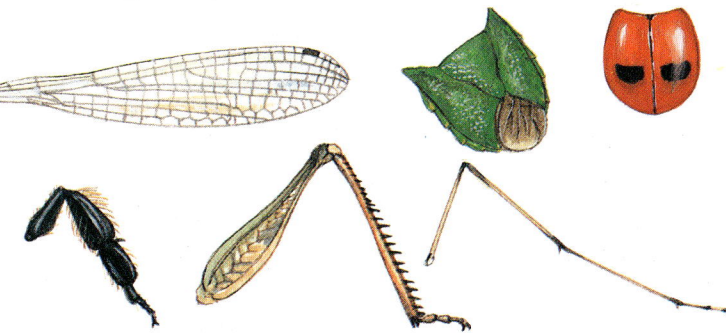

We have teeth and jaws inside our mouths to help us to eat food. Insects have jaws on the outside. A grasshopper's jaws move from side to side to cut leaves. The sharp jaws of a dragonfly are on the end of a hinge, so that they can reach forward. Bugs have pointed tubes like needles for piercing plants and other animals. The tube of a butterfly or moth is coiled up and acts like a drinking straw. Some flies have jaws like sponges for mopping up food. Can you tell which insects own these jaws?

5

Habitats

A habitat is the place where an animal lives. Insects live in all sorts of places. Look for them in the soil, under dead leaves and tree bark. You may find them on green leaves, on flowers, or just flying through the air. Some insects live in water, while others live inside people's homes.

Some insects eat dead leaves and wood. Others eat pollen and drink sugary nectar from flowers. Some suck juices from plants or nibble leaves. The carnivores catch other mini-beasts to eat.

Some larvae, like the grasshoppers shown here, already look like tiny adults. The grasshopper larva eats and grows. When its skin gets too tight, the skin splits and the larva leaves it behind. It has a new skin underneath. When its skin splits for the last time, out comes the adult grasshopper. In this book all insects on pages 8 to 15 have this kind of life cycle.

life cycle of a grasshopper ▼

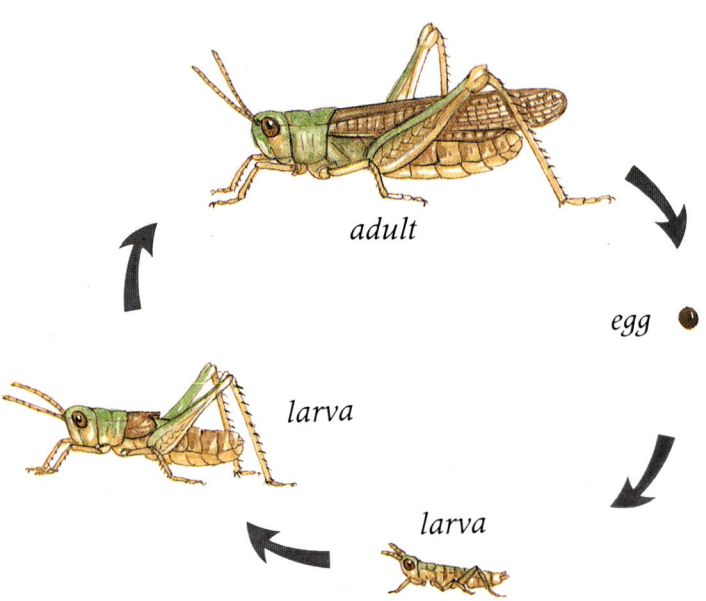

life cycle of a small white butterfly ▼

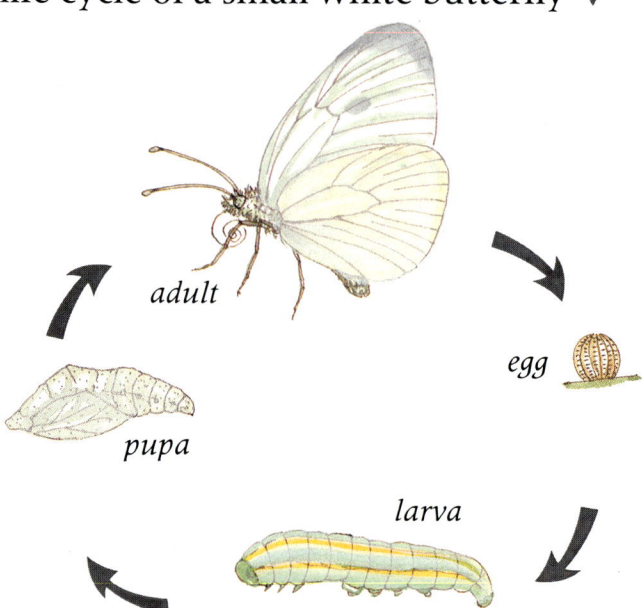

From egg to adult

Insects lay eggs on plants or animals which the newly hatched insects will eat. These young insects are called larvae. Many larvae are eaten by other animals and never become adults.

The life cycle of other insects is different. For example, the eggs of the small white butterfly hatch out into tiny larvae called caterpillars. The caterpillars look nothing like their parents. Each one grows, and splits out of its skin a few times, and then becomes a pupa (also known as a chrysalis), inside a case or cocoon. Although the pupa doesn't move, amazing changes take place inside. At last, the skin splits again and out comes an adult butterfly. In this book, all insects on pages 16 to 27 have this kind of life cycle.

Where, when and how to look

Although there are very many different kinds of insects, they may all be grouped into 'families'. Eleven families are included in this book. Look at the Contents page to find out their names.

Insects can be found everywhere! You should find insects from all eleven groups at home, in the garden, in your school grounds or your nearest park. You may not find as many in winter or early spring, as insects need warmth. The best time to look is from April until October.

furniture beetle 4mm
black ant 5mm
ladybird 6mm
housefly 7mm
mayfly 7mm
shield bug 12mm
pond skater 12mm
earwig 13mm
common field grasshopper 20mm
violet ground beetle 28mm
peppered moth (wingspan) 45mm

When you find a mini-beast, first work out if it is an insect. Look for a segmented body, wings and six legs. Try to draw it.

Then look through this book to find which picture your insect is most like. There may not be a picture exactly the same but you should find something quite close. You will then know whether your insect belongs to, say, the moth group or the beetle group. These drawings show the real sizes of some of the insects.

When you find an insect, you may want to catch it to see it more clearly. You will need an insect watcher's kit to do this. Turn to page 28 to find out how to make and use it.

REMEMBER the insect watcher's code

1. Don't collect an insect if you can see it clearly anyway. Dragonflies, for example, can be watched without being caught.
2. After looking at an insect, carefully put it back where you found it. Always put caterpillars back on the same plant.
3. Don't collect yellow and black-striped insects unless you know what they are. Remember that bees and wasps can sting!
4. ALWAYS go with an adult if hunting for water insects. Don't dip at steep banksides, trample banks, or stir up mud at the bottom of a pond. Wash your hands with tap water as soon as you can after dipping, especially before eating.

Insects are exciting to watch. Many are very colourful. Although some are pests, most are harmless and some are very useful to us. Use this book to find out about some of our common insects. Try some of the activities to learn more about the fascinating world of insects.

Grasshoppers and friends

There are many insects people often overlook. Some like springtails, are very small. Others, like earwigs and grasshoppers, are difficult to see because they hide in long grass and dense bushes.

You may need to catch a grasshopper to see it properly. Look for its large back legs for jumping, and its short antennae.

▼ Meadow grasshoppers chirrup loudly from long grass on warm, summer days. They do this by rubbing their back legs against their wings.

Bush crickets are very like grasshoppers ▶ except that they have very long antennae and only come out at night. Only male bush crickets can sing. This speckled bush cricket is difficult to spot because it hides in bushes and hedgerows.

female
male

▲ During the day earwigs squeeze into gaps under tree bark or inside hollow plant stems. At night they come out to nibble plants and catch small animals. Their fierce-looking pincers are used as weapons against shrews and other animals looking for a tasty meal.

▲ Silverfish have three hairy tails and no wings. They live in damp buildings, including houses. Look for them at night when they search for bits of paper and scraps of food.

Habits and habitats

These insects are all very different, but they do have one thing in common. They all lay eggs which hatch into larvae which look like little adults.

Many of the smaller insects have important jobs as nature's rubbish collectors. In the soil, among rotting wood and dead leaves, millions of tiny springtails are hard at work. Spread out some dead leaves on a white tray and you may just see them jumping.

Amazing insect facts

Grasshoppers have ears on their abdomen. The ears of a bush cricket are on its back legs!

The earwig is unlikely to crawl into your ear. In the old days, people slept on straw mattresses where earwigs would have lived. At night, perhaps some crept out and tickled a few ears, so giving rise to their name.

Dragonflies and Mayflies

Dragonflies are large fast-flying insects. The dragonfly group includes the smaller damselflies, but not the drabber mayfly (although the two are related). They all lay their eggs in water where their larvae will grow.

The larvae emerge at night. Their skins split to let out the adult insects, which have to dry their wings in the sunshine before they can fly.

▼ Large dragonflies, like this common hawker, catch flying insects and hold them with their front legs while they eat them. Some are called darting dragonflies. They dart from a perch to catch insects, then dart back.

The head of a dragonfly consists ▶ mainly of two large eyes. Each is made up of thousands of tiny eyes. With these the dragonfly can see everything around it at the same time. Such good eyesight helps with catching prey but makes it very difficult for us to get close to these fast moving insects.

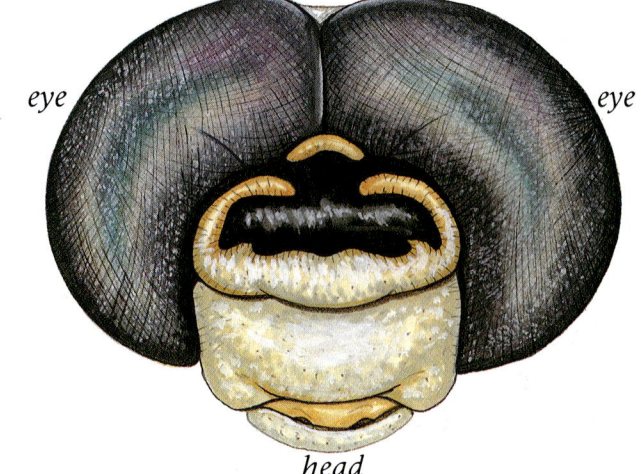

eye *eye*

head

▲ Damselflies cannot fly as fast as true dragonflies, but they too catch insects. They fold their wings back when they are resting. Sometimes two damselflies fly around together. The male large red damselflies hold their females while they lay eggs in the water.

▲ In May and June, you may see large numbers of delicate mayflies dancing over the surface of ponds.

Habits and habitats

Look for all these insects near ponds, streams and rivers. Dragonflies will fly a long way from water but always return to it to lay their eggs.

You will have to go pond-dipping to see dragonfly and mayfly larvae. A dragonfly larva has a pair of jaws on a hinge, which it can shoot forward to catch mayflies and other insects.

Amazing insect facts

Large dragonflies live for up to two years underwater before emerging. The larvae swim by jet propulsion. When they want to move quickly, they squeeze water out of their bodies and shoot forward.

Adult dragonflies live for two or three months. Adult mayflies cannot eat and live for only one or two days at the most.

Land Bugs

Insects are often called bugs, but there is one group of insects whose proper name this is. They all have needle-like beaks which they use for sucking. Like grasshoppers and dragonflies, the young bugs look like tiny adults.

▼ Look for shield bugs in the spring or autumn. This hawthorn shield bug can be found on the leaves of trees or in long grass. Shield bugs are also called stinkbugs because they produce a smelly liquid when disturbed.

Many bugs, like the common green ▶ capsid, feed on trees, grass, nettles and other plants. Look for this capsid bug from May to October, moving quickly on its long legs. It can be found on the umbrella-like flower heads of plants such as cow parsley and hogweed.

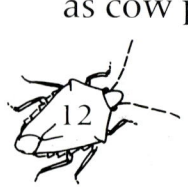

Habits and habitats

Aphids, like the greenfly below, give birth to live young instead of laying eggs. They do this every day in the spring and summer so that large numbers appear on plants. Gardeners dislike them because they suck plant juices and spread disease from plant to plant.

▲ This bug looks like a little brown frog. Froghoppers are good jumpers. They hold their wings over their back like a roof.

▲ Some tiny pear-shaped aphids are called blackfly, greenfly or whitefly, according to their colour. You may find large numbers of them on some plants. In spring most aphids have no wings. In summer look for those with wings that can fly to other plants.

Amazing insect facts

When feeding on trees such as the lime and sycamore, aphids often produce a sticky honeydew. This sugar attracts bees and ants.

In June, at the same time as the cuckoo is calling, look for frothy bubbles on grass stems known as cuckoo spit. Hiding inside will be young froghoppers. They make the froth by mixing air with plant juices.

Water Bugs

There are a number of bugs which live in fresh water. Some can walk on water and one has its own built-in snorkel. Young water bugs also live in the water and look very like their parents, only smaller.

▼ The greater water boatman swims upside down. Because of this it is also called the backswimmer. Be careful if you handle this insect as it can nip your fingers!

The smaller lesser water boatman ▶ swims the right way up. It feeds on dead and decaying plants and animals.

▼ This fierce-looking water scorpion creeps slowly over mud and water plants in shallow water. Although it looks like a scorpion, it is really just a large water bug. The pincer-like front legs are used for catching prey, including young damselflies.

▼ Look for the pond skater skimming fast across the water surface. It is searching for stranded insects. Like most water bugs, pond skaters can leave the water and fly elsewhere.

The water measurer also lives on the water surface. It has a long, thin head and stick-like body. It moves very slowly.

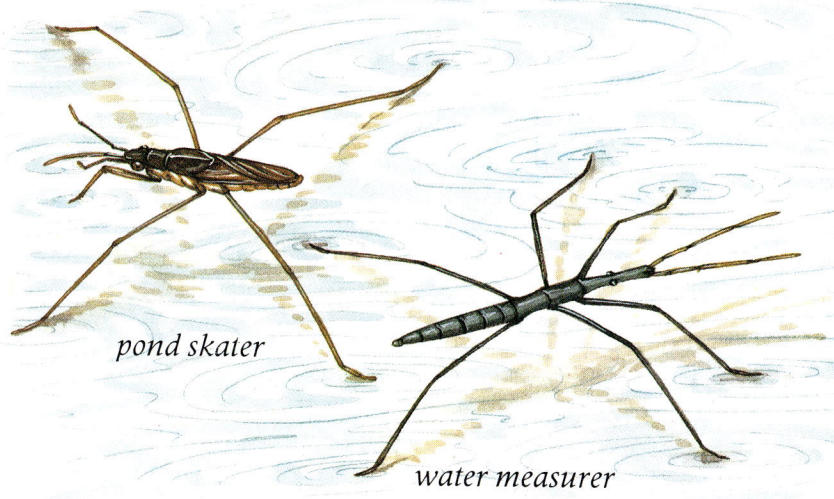

pond skater

water measurer

Habits and habitats

▼ Look for water bugs in still ponds and at the weedy edges of streams.

Most water bugs are fierce carnivores. They use beak-like jaws to pierce their prey and suck out the juice.

Amazing insect facts

Some insects can walk on water because they have very light bodies. They also have hairs on their legs to trap air and spread the weight.

Water boatmen trap air at the surface among the hairs under their bodies. If they stop swimming, the air bubbles float them back to the surface.

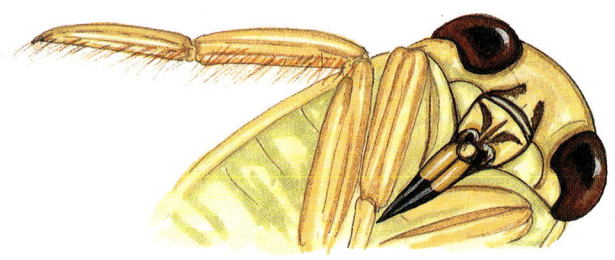

Butterflies

Like moths, butterflies have large wings covered with tiny scales. The wings are brightly coloured to attract other butterflies. Unlike moths, butterflies have antennae which are smooth and end in little clubs. The larvae of both butterflies and moths are called caterpillars.

▲ All butterflies feed on sugary nectar from flowers, which they suck up through a long coiled tube. From March to September, look for the peacock butterfly feeding on butterfly bushes, and other garden plants such as michaelmas daisies. The wings have big false eyes to frighten off birds, but are plain on the undersides. When the peacock's wings are closed, it is difficult to see the butterfly.

▲ The caterpillars of the small white feed on cabbages and similar plants. These butterflies fly from April until October. The black and white marks of white butterflies warn birds that they are poisonous.

▲ The meadow brown is the most common butterfly in the countryside. From June to September you can often get very close to it as it is a lazy flier. The caterpillars of all brown butterflies feed on grasses.

female *male* *male*

▲ All blue butterflies are small, fast fliers. The males have bright blue wings, while the females have only a small patch of blue on their wings near their body. The caterpillars of the common blue feed on a plant called bird's foot trefoil and on clover. The adults can be seen throughout the British Isles in grassy places from May until September.

Habits and habitats

Adult butterflies fly only during the spring and summer. They like warm weather so there are fewer types in northern Britain. Look for their caterpillars on food plants like the nettle. These are the caterpillars of the small tortoiseshell.

▼ Most butterflies spend the winter as caterpillars or pupae, but some hibernate as adults. So, you may see one on a warm February day.

Amazing insect facts

When a butterfly is at rest, its brightly coloured wings are folded above its body so that only the dull undersides can be seen. This helps to camouflage it from birds.

Some butterflies can fly very long distances. Red admirals come to Britain from southern Europe; painted ladies come even further from north Africa.

Moths

Moths are close relatives of butterflies, although there are many more types of them. Most fly at night and are less colourful. You will find moths in spring and summer by walking around your garden with a torch just as it gets dark. On warm evenings moths may fly into your bedroom, attracted by the light.

The large hawkmoths have fat bodies and pointed wings. They are amongst the largest moths you can find and are often bright with stripes or eyespots.

moth emerging from cocoon

▲ The six spot burnet moth flies during the day. It has fine antennae like a butterfly, and is quite colourful.

▲ Most large hawkmoths are found mainly in southern Britain, while this common poplar hawkmoth is more widespread. During the day, look for it camouflaged on a tree trunk. When disturbed, it shows a flash of red on its back wings. It flies between May and September.

▲ In the day-time, the angleshades moth looks like a dead leaf lying on the ground. Like other night-flying moths, it uses its feathery antennae to find flowers and other moths. It may be seen in gardens from May until October.

Habits and habitats

Because most moths fly at night, they have to hide from birds during the day. Many are camouflaged to look like bark, leaves or even bird droppings. Some caterpillars look like twigs. The peppered moth is the master of disguise. The light form hides on the moss and lichen-covered bark of trees. Where the air is dirty, tree trunks can be black with soot. Then the dark form is more common.

Amazing insect facts

Some male moths can smell a female a couple of kilometres away!

The winter moth is one of the few insects to fly around during the coldest months. You may see it outside your window even in January. It can do this because only the caterpillar eats; the adult does not have to find food.

▲ The large yellow underwing moth flashes its yellow back wings if disturbed.

Flies

Many insects are called flies — for example, butterflies and dragonflies. Can you think of any others? Unlike these, true flies have only one pair of flying wings. If you look at a fly carefully you can just see another pair, but these tiny, lollipop-shaped wings cannot help the insect to fly. They are used for balancing while the fly performs amazing aerobatics. Some flies can hover or even fly backwards.

▲ The daddy-long-legs, or cranefly, has a long, thin body and narrow wings. It has long legs which can easily break off if caught. The cranefly larvae, also called leather-jackets, live in the soil and eat the roots of plants.

▲ Harmless hoverflies also often look like bees or wasps. In the summer when these flies are common, young birds learn that black and yellow stripes mean danger. The adults feed on nectar, often from the large flower heads of flowers such as the hogweed. The larvae help gardeners by eating aphids.

▲ The extraordinary beefly looks just like a bee as it sucks nectar up through its long tongue. Because of this birds leave it alone, even though it is harmless.

▲ A number of flies are attracted to houses. That loud buzz at the windowpane could be a bluebottle, whose larvae feed on meat. The larvae, or maggots, of the housefly feed on kitchen rubbish and can carry diseases. The clusterfly lays its eggs in the soil and its maggots feed on worms, but on sunny days it settles on outside walls. During winter, it may hibernate in a loft and then appear inside the house.

Habits and habitats

Flies can be found everywhere, sucking up juices from decaying plants and animals, as well as eating nectar. Some flies have young that live in water. While the adult female mosquitoes suck blood from mammals, the larvae filter food from the water. Midge larvae are often bright red and so are called bloodworms. They live in tubes in the mud of ponds or rivers.

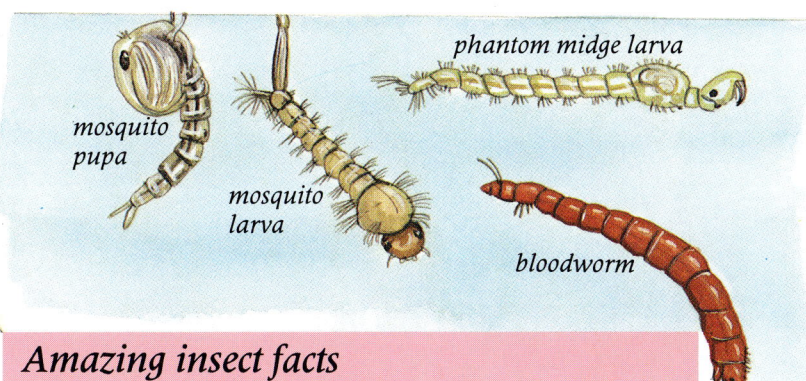

Amazing insect facts

The larva of the phantom midge is see-through. It hangs in the water with little air sacs like swimming arm-bands, ready to surprise other small animals which it eats.

Some flies are so small that their larvae can live inside leaves. If you find a holly tree, look for yellow blotches on the leaves. The holly leaf miner eats away, snug in the warmth of the leaf, from September until May. Then the tiny fly comes out through a small hole.

Bees, Wasps and Ants

Many insects which belong to this group are very useful to us. They are often brightly coloured. The bold black and yellow stripes of bees and wasps mean Danger! I sting. However, neither insect will sting unless annoyed.

▼ Adult wasps feed mainly on nectar, fruit and other sweet things. They usually nest underground, often in holes made by mice. Worker wasps collect pieces of wood and make their nest, or colony, out of paper. Up to 2000 wasps can live in the nest, but only the queen survives the winter. A wasp's sting is used as a weapon to kill other insects. In the garden, wasps can be very useful as they kill caterpillars and aphids to feed their larvae.

Bumblebee queens live underground ▶ during the winter. These colourful, hairy bees then lay eggs and start a colony of up to 150 bees. Like honeybees, bumblebees are useful because they carry pollen from flower to flower. This is called pollination and without it many plants, trees and crops would not produce seeds and fruits.

▲ Most honeybees are kept in hives. There can be up to 50,000 bees in a hive, or colony, and many survive over winter. In the spring, worker bees busily collect nectar and pollen in special baskets on their legs. Honey is made in the hive to feed the larvae and to feed the bees during the following winter.

winged queen *worker*

▲ Look for black ants in your garden under paving slabs or in the lawn. The workers have no wings and may march into your house looking for sugary foods. At the end of the summer, you may see the queen ants when they fly.

Habits and habitats

Unlike ants, bumblebees and honeybees, most British wasps live alone. Some cause growths called galls on plants when they lay their eggs.

▼ On oak leaves, the common spangle galls fall to the ground with the leaves in autumn. The tiny adult wasp then flies out in the spring. Other wasps make galls of different shapes.

Amazing insect facts

Most ants are farmers, 'milking' sweet honeydew from aphids. Some actually keep aphid eggs and put them on plants in the spring. They protect aphids against ladybirds and other insects.

Cuckoo bumblebees do not make their own nest. Instead, they find other bumblebees' nests, kill the queens, and lay their own eggs. The bumblebees then bring up the larvae of the cuckoo bee!

Larger Beetles

From the smallest to the largest beetle, all have some features in common. They have hard front wings, which form a case for the back ones, which are used for flying. They also all have sharp jaws for biting. Some beetles catch other animals, some chew plants and others eat dead plants and animals.

▼ Ground beetles run fast on long legs to catch other insects at night. This very large violet ground beetle has black and violet wingcases joined together so that it cannot fly. Look for ground beetles under stones and logs and among dead leaves. They are very helpful to gardeners as they eat many pests.

The long, thin, black, devil's coach horse ▶ beetle is one of many insects known as rove beetles. It looks rather like an earwig and is often found inside houses. It can fly, but like an earwig, it folds its wings over many times so that they can be covered by two little flaps. When disturbed, it raises its back like a scorpion and snaps its jaws. It is harmless to humans but deadly to slugs and small insects.

▼ The stag beetle is Britain's largest beetle. The male has huge jaw-like antlers which are just for show, while the smaller female has jaws which can nip. However, neither needs to eat. You may see them flying on warm summer evenings.

▼ The cockchafer is also called the maybug, because it flies in May and June. It is a heavy beetle with reddish-brown wingcases. Cockchafers often hit window panes in the early evening, having been attracted to them by lights inside. The larvae feed on roots, and the adults on the leaves of the trees.

Habits and habitats

There are more than 4000 types of beetle in Britain. Many larger beetles live in woods among logs and leaves. They make a good meal for birds, badgers and even foxes.

The larvae of the lesser stag beetle eat away inside rotting wood for three or four years. Woodpeckers often visit trees to feed on these soft larvae.

Amazing insect facts

Burying beetles lay their eggs on a dead bird, or a small mammal like a mouse. To hide the food from other insects, they then bury the dead animal, which may be much bigger than themselves. They do this by digging the soil from beneath the bird or mammal.

Smaller Beetles

Some beetles are very useful. Ladybirds, for example, eat large numbers of aphids which harm plants and crops. Other beetles can do damage by eating plants and wood.

▼ This bright red beetle is called the soldier beetle because in the old days soldiers wore uniforms of the same colour. Its bright colours, like the black and red or yellow of a ladybird, warn birds that it contains a poison and is nasty to eat. Look for it from May until August feeding on insects which live on large flowers.

Some beetles live part, or all of their lives ▶ in water. The yellow and black diving beetle can be found all through the year in small streams. The non-stop whirligig beetle spins on the surface of ponds, but can also dive below.

▲ Our commonest ladybird has seven spots, but there are many other types. The smaller twenty-two spot ladybird is yellow and black. The two spot ladybird is usually red with two black spots, but this black beetle with six spots is also a two spot ladybird!

Habits and habitats

Many beetles, large and small, feed on wood. Often this is useful, helping it to rot down into the soil. However, if the wood is inside a house, it is not so good. The tiny larvae of the furniture beetle are called woodworm. They eat wooden beams and furniture. Often you do not know they are there until the adults come out from little holes, or a chair leg breaks!

furniture beetle

elm bark beetle

Amazing insect facts

Over 25 million trees may have died in Britain from Dutch Elm Disease. This disease is carried by the tiny elm bark beetle whose larvae eat tracks under the bark. You may not find the beetles themselves, but look for pieces of bark under dead elm trees.

In the spring, look for long brown click beetles with short legs. When disturbed they may fall to the ground and act dead. They arch their backs and, with a loud click, spring into the air. They keep doing this until they land on their feet.

▲There are many tiny beetles called weevils. They have a long snout with jaws at the end. They are all vegetarians and many are pests. Nettles are good plants on which to look for them. This large green weevil is only seen in May and June, but look out for other types.

Activities

Insect watcher's kit

Small margarine tubs with see-through lids are useful for holding and looking at insects. Small insects can be put in the see-through tubes in which some photographic films are sold.

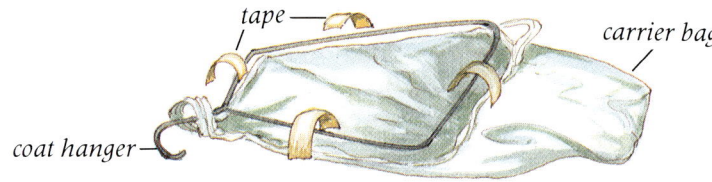

Make a sweep net by pulling a wire coat-hanger into a square and taping it to a plastic carrier bag.

A pooter will help you to suck up small insects you want to look at. Attach two straws to a length of polythene tubing with a small piece of muslin. The muslin will stop the insects going into your mouth!

Make a pond-dipping net by attaching a flour sieve or small aquarium net to a lenth of cane. You will also need a spoon to pick up your animals, and a large ice-cream tub or pie dish to make a sort of aquarium.

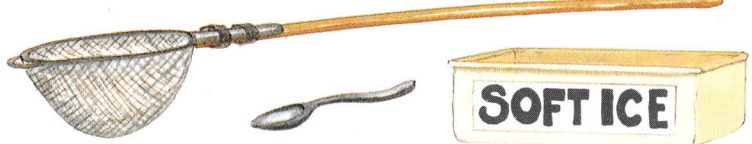

Spring

In spring you can look for water insects, particularly young insects. Remember the insect watcher's code (page 7), and approach the pond slowly and quietly. Can you see any animals living on the surface?

TAKE CARE!

Half fill your white tub with clear pond water. Quickly sweep your pond net through the water, and turn it out into the tub. Carefully remove any stones or pieces of plant so you can see the insects more clearly against the white background.

Find out which insects live where by sweeping in different places: on the pond surface; among the plants at the edge; under the water; and at the bottom of the pond. Make sure you put all your animals back carefully.

28

From the beginning of June, look among the plants at a pond's edge and you may find the skins of dragonflies, damselflies or mayflies. The young insects will have climbed out of the water, shed their skins and flown away.

Now you will also find more land insects. Carefully move your sweep net backwards and forwards in the long dry grass, collecting the insects in tubes, or in a pooter if they are small.

Hold an umbrella upside down under the branch of a tree. Tap the branch a few times with a stick and collect the falling insects in the umbrella. Now you can find out which insects live in this kind of tree.

Summer

Summer is the time to keep caterpillars and watch them turn into butterflies. Find a large plastic ice-cream box, line it with kitchen paper and fit it with a muslin cover. Place some fresh leaves in the box for food. Use cabbage or cauliflower leaves for white butterflies, and nettles for peacocks and small tortoiseshells. Make sure you handle the nettles carefully!

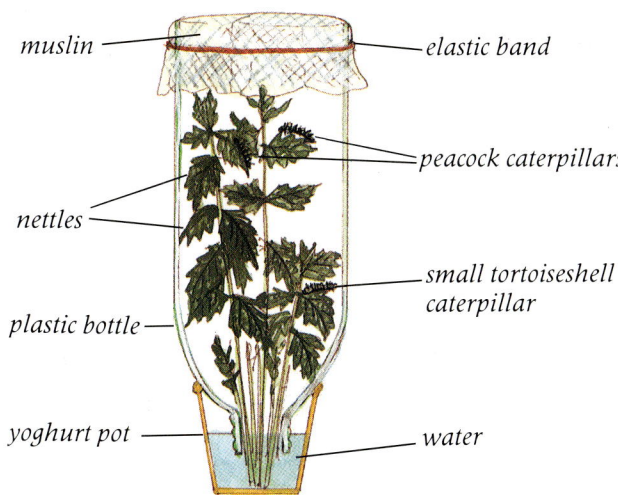

You can also use an upturned plastic bottle with the plant stems in a pot of water underneath. This way you will not need to change the food so often.

It is easy to spot butterfly caterpillars on nettles because they cluster together. Look for green, or green and yellow caterpillars on vegetables such as cabbage. These are the young small, and large white butterflies. Use a paint brush carefully to lift about ten small or two large caterpillars into their new home. Remember to change the food every few days. Each caterpillar will turn into a chrysalis before the butterfly emerges. Never disturb the caterpillars while this is happening and keep the container in the shade.

You can find out a lot about insects just by watching them. Find a plant which has aphids such as greenfly on it. Do ants visit to collect the sugary honeydew made by the greenfly? Do ladybirds eat the aphids? Watch a patch of colourful flowers. Can you see bees collecting nectar and pollen? Which flowers are visited most? Do they have a strong scent? Are they brightly coloured?

You can make your garden attractive to butterflies by growing plants such as buddleia (the butterfly bush) and michaelmas daisies. If you have a wild area with the plants caterpillars need, the butterflies will stay and lay eggs. Nettles, long grass and wild flowers all encourage butterflies to lay eggs. You can buy wild flower seeds to sow in September.

In the summer, you can look for night-flying insects such as moths. Make a special 'drink' to attract moths by mixing one tablespoon of black treacle with two tablespoons of sugar and two tablespoons of water. Ask an adult to heat the mixture in a pan until it thickens. Leave it to cool. Just before dark, soak a piece of cloth in the mixture and pin it to a tree trunk or fence post. Make sure the cloth is sheltered from the wind. Leave it for a while and when you return, if it is a warm evening, you will find moths drinking the sugar through their coiled tubes. (Although the sugar and treacle mixture is very sticky, the moths do not get stuck.)

Autumn and Winter

You can also encourage butterflies to your garden by putting old apples on the lawn in autumn. The butterflies suck up the sweet liquid made as the apples rot.

If you find a butterfly inside the house in winter, don't let it fly outside. Put it in a cool shed or garage where it will go back to sleep until spring.

By winter, many insects are hiding away until the following spring. Earwigs may be found in the hollow stems of dead plants such as runner beans. Tiny beetles and springtails hide in pine cones, and other insects can be found under the bark of old logs. Cracks around window frames are a favourite spot for ladybirds. Look under logs and stones, but make sure you put them down again in the same place.

To find insects that are still active, dig a small hole in the ground near logs or a compost heap. Bury a plastic cup up to the rim. Make a roof with a piece of tile or board to keep the animals dry. Beetles and other insects may fall in, especially at night. A piece of meat or cheese may tempt different sorts of insects into your trap. Never leave the animals too long and always let them go carefully.

a pitfall trap

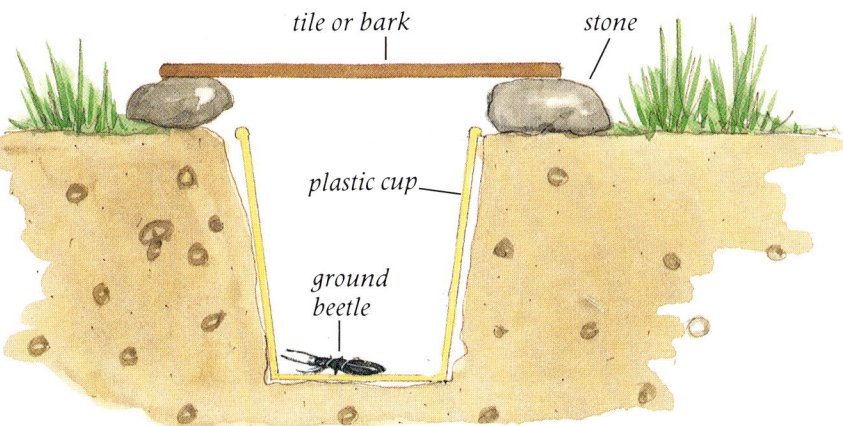

If you have enjoyed reading this book, why not join WATCH, the national wildlife and enviroment club for children? Each year WATCH organises exciting projects on wildlife and conservation for all the family through a network of WATCH groups. In your area these are run by your local Wildlife Trust. For a membership leaflet and more information write to:

WATCH
The Royal Society of Nature Conservation (RSNC)
Witham Park
Waterside South
Lincoln LN5 7JN

Index

This index to all the species of insects, does not contain the names of the insect groups covered by this book. Each of these is listed on the Contents page (p.3).

angleshades moth 18
aphid 13, 22, 23, 26, 29

beefly 20
blackfly 13
bloodworms 21
bluebottle 21
bumblebee 22, 23
burying beetle 25

click beetle 27
clusterfly 21
cockchafer 25
common blue butterfly 17
common green capsid bug 12
common hawker dragonfly 10
common wasp 22
cranefly 20
cuckoo bumblebees 23

daddy-long-legs 20
devil's coach horse beetle 24
diving beetle 26

earwigs 8, 9, 31
elm bark beetle 27

froghopper 13
furniture beetle 27

gall 23
greater water boatman 14
greenfly 13
ground beetle 24

hawthorn shield bug 12
holly leaf miner 21
honeybee 22, 23
housefly 21
hoverfly 20

ladybird 23, 26, 27, 31
large red damselfly 11
large white butterfly 29, 30
large yellow underwing moth 19
leather-jackets 20
lesser stag beetle 25
lesser water boatman 14, 15

maybug 25
meadow brown butterfly 17
meadow grasshopper 8
midge larvae 21, 29
mosquito 21

painted lady butterfly 17
peacock butterfly 16, 30
peppered moth 19
phantom midge larva 21
pond skater 15
poplar hawkmoth 18

red admiral butterfly 17, 30

seven spot ladybird 27
silverfish 9
six spot burnet moth 18
small tortoiseshell butterfly 17, 30
small white butterfly 16, 29
soldier beetle 26
speckled bush cricket 8
springtail 8, 30, 31
stag beetle 25
stinkbugs 12

twenty-two spot ladybird 27
two spot ladybird 27

violet ground beetle 24

water measurer 15
water scorpion 15
weevil 27
whirligig beetle 26
whitefly 13
winter moth 19
woodworm 27